HELP! WHO IS THIS STRANGER IN MY HOME?

A practical guide for parents to understand and connect with their **adolescents.**

Oluwatoyin Ogunkanmi

HELP! WHO IS THIS STRANGER IN MY HOME?

ISBN: 978-978-981-776-4

Published by:
Parenting Support System,
Abuja, Nigeria
oluwatoyin@oluwatoyinogunkanmi.com

Book Designed & Printed by:
Bigshop Concepts
bigshopconcept@gmail.com
+2348132926288

National Library of Nigeria Cataloguing-in-Publication Data

TABLE OF CONTENT

DEDICATION

To my wonderful and talented sons Jaiyeolaoluwa and Tioluwani, and to my very creative and loving daughter Anjolaoluwa, I bless the day I held you all in my arms for the first time.I am richly blessed to have the privilege to raise you.

I have learnt to love more, laugh unreservedly, to love basketball, football and also to love singing because of you all. Thank you , Love you greatly.

Taiwo, My love, my coach, my greatest support system Thank you for all you are to me, thank you for being the best father ever. I have learnt more about parenting from you than from any coach, training or book. I love you.

Parenting is a journey of continuous learning, unlearning, and relearning. There are no quick fix solutions; you just have to trust the process.

--Oluwatoyin Ogunkanmi

INTRODUCTION

Parenting is a journey that involves continuous learning, unlearning, and relearning. For every stage of your child's development, you need to equip yourself with the necessary skills and information to raise him/her effectively.

The strategy and method you used when your child was a baby, a toddler, or a young child is quite different from what you will use in raising an adolescent or a young adult.

Parenting involves you promoting and supporting the spiritual, psychosocial, cognitive, emotional and moral development of your child. To raise a well-balanced adult, you have to ensure that your child is developing well in all these areas.

Parents tend to dread the time their children will be approaching the adolescent years. This is due to misinformation and myths surrounding this period of growth.

Adolescence is a period of drastic and rapid changes. These changes involve the physical, emotional, cognitive and social development of your child. It's a period of transitioning from childhood to adulthood.

Having raised two teenage boys and a preteen girl, I can confidently say that these periods also come with changes in the adolescents' behaviours.

In my line of work as a parenting coach, I have counselled and coached some parents of adolescents, and I understand the pains they go through in not knowing how to connect with their children.

As your children begin to change and develop, you also should be changing in terms of your parenting style. You are to seek new ways of parenting your adolescent, not sticking to your old ways of handling things. This will improve your relationship with them and make the transition smooth. The relationship between you and your child should change from you telling him/her what to do, to you guiding them. I want you to know that you play an important role in shaping your child's behaviour.

The secret to raising your adolescent (pre-teen or teenager) into a well-balanced adult starts with you building a trusting relationship with them, and also seeking to understand them.

When you build a trusting relationship based on rapport and understanding your adolescent, it breaks down all barriers and paves the way for a deeper connection, making your ability to influence them more effective. You need to get into their world to understand what is important to them.

During this developmental stage, your child begins to discover himself/herself, and is also seeking an independent identity from you. That is why you begin to feel alienated from them.

They are going through the identity formation stage and want to affiliate more with their peers -- their friends become important to them. Your guidance and influence are still needed, not in a controlling way, but more as suggestions.

Adolescents have emotional needs which we have to guide them to fulfil.

These needs have been divided into three, using the acronym, ABC. A stands for **Acceptance** (the need to be loved), B stands for **Belonging** (the need to be included), while C stands for **Control** (the need to be independent and in control of their decisions).

You have to guide them by giving them choices that are not life threatening, i.e. choices they can live with.

One of the things that breaks the trust in your relationship with your adolescents is when you do not believe in their abilities, or when they are being compared to other children.

Every child God has given to you is unique, including your teenager. In seeking to understand them, you have to identify and accept their uniqueness. Your child's uniqueness involves the way he/she responds to the environment, the way they respond to love, how they prefer to learn, and the different intelligences God has placed in them. (I have written a whole chapter on identifying your child's uniqueness).

Connecting with your adolescent becomes easier when you step into their world, get to know them better, and become interested in what they like.

Discipline at this level takes a whole different dimension. It is not about you controlling their behaviour, but about you becoming deliberate in teaching, dialoguing, reasoning, influencing and coaching. (You will be doing more coaching during this developmental stage.)

When correcting your adolescent, avoid doing so in anger. Discipline that is effective is one that is done in love -- one that is fair, firm and consistent. Please note that discipline is different from punishment. (I wrote about this difference in my book, **Smart Parenting.**) Your best tools during their adolescent years are your ability to advise and explain, and also to be a good role model. These will make your discipline effective.

There are some myths about teenagers and teenage years that influence the way parents raise their children. The most common of them is that teenagers are difficult to manage and raise; it makes some parents to be harsh and strict with their children. This myth is not true. What is true is that these children are going through a lot of rapid physical, emotional, psychological and social changes which may be challenging because they themselves do not understand, and these changes are making them feel uncomfortable.

They are going through a lot of hormonal changes that are affecting their emotions, leading to mood swings. (I have written some tips on how you can become your child's emotion coach).

The most important thing for teenagers at this stage of development is the stability in their homes, and unconditional love from their parents. At the root of most teenage misbehaviours is an emotional need for love and connection. If their emotional tank is full, the rate of misbehaviour in them will reduce.

Parental guidance and influence are very important during the adolescent years; most life mistakes are actually made during this life stage. If the adolescent is not properly guided but left to discover life for himself, he/she might end up making some costly mistakes that will affect him/her all through life.

Your adolescent needs you to understand and connect with them better. They want your guidance and influence; but if you are not speaking their language, how can you connect or influence? (I have written some great tips on how to communicate effectively with your adolescent).

As parents of adolescents, you have to develop a great relationship with them to make your influence more effective in their lives. **Your friendship is a very vital tool.**

In this book, I will be discussing the cognitive (brain) development of adolescents and how it affects their decision-making process. I will also be shedding light on their emotional and mental wellness; this area of their lives is as important as their physical wellbeing. Your love and support have a direct, positive impact on their mental health.

There are some conversations we need to have with our children, which I have written about in this book. These conversations include sex, faith, money, alcohol, drugs, moral development, and their career.

These conversations should be ongoing, and not just a one-off thing. From my experience in raising my children and as a parenting coach, I will tell you that having the following qualities will go a long way in making your parenting journey smooth:

1. Loving unconditionally.

2. Having empathy.

3. Respecting your child's individuality.

4. Being kind and gentle towards your child.

5. Having lots of patience.

6. Exercising lots of self-control.

Finally, I will be sharing essential life skills, values, and pillars of character which you need to teach your adolescents. These life skills are to prepare them for adulthood -- preparing them to become responsible and independent adults.

Your home is a preparatory ground like the quiver in Psalm 127, and your children are arrows in the hands of the Lord -- arrows that you need to prepare properly before launching them into the world. Adolescence is the best time for you to prepare your child for adulthood. One thing I say often is that you need to start with the end in mind. What type of adult do you want to raise? What type of person are you raising now? When your children are celebrating you on your 80th birthday, what type of parent will they say you were (when they were adolescents)?

Start by creating your parenting vision and plan. Set parenting goals for each child, some of which should be raising a person that has an independent mind, critical thinking skills, self-confidence, and empathy for others.

This book is a practical guide and a great resource for parents of adolescents on how they can equip themselves with new skills to understand, connect and prepare their adolescents to become well-balanced adults.

Thank you for your purchase!

CHAPTER 1

HELP! WHO IS THIS STRANGER IN MY HOME?

'We worry about what a child will become tomorrow, yet we forget that he is someone today.' — *Stacia Tauscher*

One day, you wake up and realise that your sweet, cute little child who was always cuddling up to you, asking for hugs or kisses has turned into a different person who is frequently having mood swings, seeking independence, and not wanting to spend time with you or his/her siblings, but prefers the company of friends!

You are wondering where your baby went, and who the stranger in your home is. That stranger is your adolescent who is seeking to understand the drastic changes happening to him/her, who is also crying for help, but in a dramatic way.

The transition from childhood to adolescence for my older son was quite seamless and with no drama. When my younger son became an adolescent, I assumed it would be without drama like that of his older brother, since he is a friendly and loving person. Instead, I had a grumpy young boy who was just keeping to himself or his room, and I noticed we were drifting apart -- no more 'Mummy, please, may I hug you?' He began snapping at his younger sister who used to be his buddy.

Whenever he felt we were not understanding him or he felt frustrated, he would just pick his ball and go outside to kick as a way of easing off tension and frustration.

This became frustrating to me as I knew I had done a great job in his younger years, yet I was not connecting with him. So, in my usual way, I had to seek counsel. I spoke to my senior partner on this journey of parenting -- God. I got some direction about studying adolescents and their peculiarities.

In my book, **Smart Parenting**, I wrote that smart parenting starts with you being in a partnership with God, because He has given these children to you and He knows how best you are to raise them.

My study and research on Adolescence Psychology gave me a whole lot of insight into what was happening with my son and many other adolescents. I had a conversation with him and many revelations came out.

The first insight is that when children reach this stage of development, many changes might happen. These changes and their effects are different for each child. Each child is unique and different. You might have the same family rules in the home, but the strategy or method you will use in raising each child might be different because of their uniqueness.

WHAT IS ADOLESCENCE?

Adolescence refers to the period of human growth that occurs between childhood and adulthood. It comes with lots of drastic changes in the adolescent, and it's a season of fast-paced development in these key areas: physical, cognitive, emotional and psychosocial. This developmental stage begins at around age 10 and ends around age 21. Adolescence can be divided into three stages: early adolescence

(10-15), middle adolescence (14-17) and late adolescence (17-21).

Below is a table showing the characteristics of each stage of adolescence:

Diagram: World Health Organization 2010

	EARLY 10-15 years	MIDDLE 14-17 years	LATE 16-19 years
Growth of body	• Secondary sexual characteristics appear • Rapid growth reaches a peak	▢ Secondary sexual characteristics advance ▢ Growth slows down ▢ Has reached approximately 95% of adult	▢ Physically mature

		growth	
Growth of brain (Prefrontal cortex)	•	▢ Brain growth occurs ▢ Influence on social and problem-solving skills	▢
Cognition (ability to get knowledge through different ways of thinking)	• Uses concrete thinking ('here and now') • Does not understand how a present action has result in the	▢ Thinking can be more abstract (theoretical) but goes back to concrete thinking under stress	▢ Most thinking is now abstract ▢ Plans for the future ▢ Understands how choices and decisions

	future	▪ Better understands results of own actions ▪ Very self-absorbed	now have an affect on the future
Psychological and social	• Spends time thinking about rapid physical growth and body image (how others see them) • Frequent changes in mood	▪ Creates their body image ▪ Thinks a lot about impractical or impossible dreams ▪ Feels very powerful ▪ Experimen	▪ Plans and follows long term goals ▪ Usually comfortable with own body image ▪ Understands right from wrong (morally and ethically)

		ts with sex, drugs, friends, risks	
Family	• Struggles with rules about independence/dependence • Argues and is disobedient	□ Argues with people in authority	□ Moving from a child-parent/guardian relationship to a more equal adult-adult relationship

Peer group	• Important for their development • Intense friendships with same sex • Contact with opposite sex in groups	⬚ Strong peer friendships ⬚ Peer group most important and determines behaviour	⬚ Decisions/values less influenced by peers in favour of individual friendships ⬚ Selection of partner based on individual choice rather than what others think
Sexuality	• Self-exploration and evaluation	⬚ Forms stable relationships	⬚ Mutual and balanced sexual relations

Stages of Adolescent Development

From this table, we can see that these children are really going through different changes; changes that if not prepared for or properly handled, might cause a lot of stress to them and even you, their parents.

The first thing you need to do is to get yourself equipped with practical tools and information on how to help your child to deal with these changes. Thank God you are reading this book because in the following pages,

I will be discussing the different aspects of changes and how you can help your child.

PHYSICAL DEVELOPMENT/CHANGE

I will be starting with the physical changes because they are the most prominent and the most obvious of all the changes, and the ones that give adolescents great concerns. The physical changes occurring in your adolescent start between the ages of 9 and 11. These changes might not be initially obvious until between ages 12 and 13 when the visible physical signs begin to show. However, because children of the 21st century are hitting puberty earlier, you might start seeing some of these signs in children as young as 8 years of age. My daughter started earlier than the regular 9 years. Some parents might have called it baby fat but in reality, adolescence had started.

For girls, there are signs like the budding of the breasts, the uterus expanding, and pubic hair growing on the lips of the vagina. For the boys, the testicles and the skin around the testicles (also known as scrotum) begin to get bigger, and pubic hair begins to grow at the base of the penis. Parents need to know that girls develop earlier than boys.

These developments make them appear adult-like, yet they are still emotionally immature. Below are a few physical changes that will become more obvious in both sexes:

Girls

Physical changes in girls usually start after age 12. These changes include:

- Breast 'buds' continue to grow and expand.

- Pubic hair gets thicker and curlier.

- Hair starts forming under the armpits.

- The first signs of acne may appear on the face and back.

- The highest growth rate for height begins (around 3.2 inches per year).

- Hips and thighs start to build up fat.

- Onset of menstruation. When menstruation becomes regular, they are capable of reproduction.

Boys

Physical changes in boys usually start around age 13. These changes include:

- Penis gets longer as testicles continue to grow bigger.

- Some breast tissue may start to form under the nipples (this happens to some teenage boys during development and usually goes away within a couple of years).

- Boys begin to have wet dreams (ejaculation at night).

- As the voice begins to change, it may 'crack,' going from high to lower pitches.

- Muscles get larger.

- Height growth increases to 2 to 3.2 inches per year.

- Facial hair

SENSORY AND MOTOR DEVELOPMENT

Children around this age may be a little awkward or clumsy. Their brains need time to adjust to longer limbs and bigger bodies. Getting regular moderate exercise can improve coordination and help your child build healthy habits.

Your role as a parent is to help them understand these changes even before they reach the age of puberty by...

1. Discussing with your child before he or she reaches the age of puberty, about the changes to expect. You are to prepare them upfront. For the boys, talk to them about the wet dreams, the deepening of their voices, etc. For the girls, speak about their body shape and build their self-esteem.

2. Let them know about their physical changes and the need for proper hygiene -- especially the girls during their menstrual cycle.

3. Encourage them to eat healthy, to avoid eating disorders.

4. Some adolescents might be early developers and start feeling awkward around their friends who are yet to develop. Please help them to feel comfortable with their bodies, and to have a healthy body image.

5. Your adolescent requires more rest. Ensure he or she gets the required sleep hours.

COGNITIVE DEVELOPMENT

Cognitive development involves changes in the ability of how a child thinks and reasons. The changes in your adolescent are not just physical, but also involve mental and social ones. During these years, they (adolescents) become able to think more abstractly (getting a deeper, theoretical meaning of things).

Cognitive development in adolescents is critical in preparing them to manage complexities, make judgments, and plan for their future. Please note that each child may progress at a different rate and may have a different view of the world.

Below is a summary of the abilities you may see in your adolescent:

- Develops the ability to think abstractly. Thinking about the possibilities of things. He/she starts to question what he/she is being told. (You might start hearing phrases like, 'Why, mum?' or 'What do you mean, dad?' They just need you to clarify what you are saying).

- Thinks long-term (mid adolescence).

- Is concerned with philosophy, politics, and social issues (late adolescence).

- Sets goals.

- Compares himself or herself to peers.

Neuro-imaging studies demonstrate that adolescents may experience greater emotional satisfaction with risk-taking behaviour. Some researchers have shown that adolescents have higher levels of incentive motivation (drive to engage in behaviours in anticipation of reward) than children or adults, due to heightened dopamine transmission within the brain. This satisfaction can predispose adolescents to engage in strange behaviours, despite being aware of the risks; for example, a teenager who is driving under the influence of alcohol or drugs, or one who is riding with an intoxicated driver. Another example is that of a teenager who is standing on a moving vehicle.

Studies have shown that they may be unable to link cause and effect in regard to unhealthy behaviours like smoking, overeating, alcohol, drugs, reckless driving and early sex, and may not be prepared to avoid risks.

Due to the prefrontal cortex still developing, your adolescent largely still depends on his/her emotional brain to make certain rational decisions; that's why the way they behave, solve problems or make decisions might be impulsive. (I will discuss this in more detail in the next chapter.) Adolescents are said to think with their feelings/emotions. Your role as the parent is to help encourage positive and healthy cognitive growth in your adolescent. You can use the following tips:

1. Encourage your child to share ideas and thoughts with you by including him or her in

the discussions of different issues, topics and current news. In my home, we encourage our children to listen to the daily news and ask them to discuss what is going on in the world. We also have a knowledge sharing session where we deliberately share information or discuss recently-learnt things or recently-read books.

2. Encourage your teen to think independently and develop his or her own ideas. My husband and I encourage our teenagers to come up with different business ideas, how to generate income, and how to support their community. Try the same with yours, and you will be surprised at what they will come up with. My older son launched his T-shirt business during one of their summer vacations. My younger son came up with an idea to start an NGO to teach children of low-income communities how to play football.

3. Encourage your child to set yearly goals. At the beginning of every year, our children set goals for different areas of their lives: academic, spiritual, physical, and extracurricular.

4.   Encourage your child to think about their future. Ask them questions about what they would like to change in the world. If they had all the money in the world, what would they do with their time? (Not the usual 'what do you want to be when you grow up?') Ask thought-provoking questions.

5.   Let them read books and watch movies that can give them new ideas and new ways to think. Reading helps them to expand their vocabulary and their horizon.

6.   Encourage your adolescent to have the required hours of sleep and rest to help his/her brain develop well.

7.   Compliment and praise your teen for well thought-out decisions.

8.   Help him or her in re-evaluating poorly made decisions.

Teens' abilities to question and ponder will also lead them to start questioning their own identity. They will begin to understand that they play different roles to different people, such roles as being someone's child, sibling, student, athlete, etc. They will take these different roles and their new willingness to explore other options, and try on various personas. Testing out new identities is a typical and necessary part of adolescence.

This will take us to the next developmental change in your adolescent.

PSYCHOSOCIAL DEVELOPMENT

The adolescence stage is when the child begins to discover himself; he begins to go through the different stages of identity formation. I will be using the psychosocial theory of development in humans by psychoanalyst, Erik Erikson, to discuss this stage of development in adolescents. He identified 8 stages that every human must go through to develop certain skills.

According to Erikson, identity formation, while beginning in childhood, gains prominence during adolescence. Faced with physical growth, sexual maturation and impending career choices, adolescents must accomplish the task of integrating their prior experiences while growing up and their characteristics into a stable identity. Erikson coined the phrase 'identity crisis' to describe the temporary instability and confusion adolescents experience as they struggle with alternatives and choices.

The psychosocial development period is the period your child starts to try out different styles in terms of fashion, hairstyle, even looks. One day, your son might want to grow afro hair style while the next, he would want to have his hair wavy. For the girls, they become more conscious of how they look and what they wear.

They take up different personas, searching for an identity. To cope with the uncertainties of this stage, adolescents may over identify with heroes and mentors (football heroes, musicians, actors, actresses or on-air/TV personalities), fall in love, and bond together in cliques, excluding others on the basis of real or imagined differences.

According to Erikson, successful resolution of this crisis depends on one's progress through previous developmental stages, centering on fundamental issues of trust, autonomy, and initiative. By the age of 21, about half of all adolescents are thought to have resolved their identity crises, and are ready to move on to the adult challenges of love and work. However, those who are not able to resolve their identity crises end up having role confusion.

The first area of adolescent psychosocial development is the establishment of independence. This occurs when the adolescent strives to become emotionally independent from parents or authority figures. During the early and middle adolescent years, there are usually more frequent conflicts between teens and their parents. Often, this is because the youths are trying to assert their individuality and are exercising their independence. He or she prefers to spend more time with friends, or alone. These friends might replace parents as sources of advice.

Do not be upset when your adolescent prefers the company of his/her friends to yours (they want to affiliate and belong to their peer group) or might want to spend more time alone in their room. (They are just seeking independence from you). You are to guide them with the selection of friends by teaching your family values and getting to know who their friends are.

One of the things we did in my home was for us to get interested in our adolescents' friends, took them all out during some weekends for movies; we offered carpooling, invited them for sports activities like football, paintball, go-karting and basketball games. This was for us to know who their friends are, and also to get to know their (friends') parents.

Do not stop them from interacting with their friends or bringing their friends home, because you won't be able to correct or guide them when they pick the wrong ones.

The struggle for independence begins during early adolescence (between ages 10-12 years), which is characterized by forming same-sex peer groups.

This was the first mistake I made when I started teaching my pre-teens in church; I did not know of this characteristic of early adolescence. I would separate the girls and the boys, forming cliques in class so that I could maintain order. But unknown to me, it was upsetting their clique formation.

During this time, adolescents are concerned with how they appear before others. Their peer group, which is typically same-sex, is often idealized and has a strong influence on the adolescents' development. As a result, adolescents may use clothing, hairstyles, language, and other accessories to fit in with their peers. During middle adolescence, the peer group becomes a mixed sex peer group, and assumes a primary social role for the adolescent. Adolescents begin to have short, intense love relationships, while looking for the 'ideal' partner. It is also not uncommon for adolescents to have crushes during this stage. (My boys had different cases of crushes that I had to listen to and give advice on).

When your children come to you to discuss their crushes, you are not to shut them up, exclaim, shout, or punish them. If you do this, you will be sending them away and closing the door for further, deeper and serious conversations.

You should have started the sex conversation before this stage. In my e-book, **Talking About Sex**, I have practical tips on how to start the sex conversation with your children. Sexuality conversations should be ongoing, not a one-off thing.

Family conflict is likely to be at its peak at this stage. As adolescents' independent functioning increases, they may examine their personal experiences, relate their experience to others, and develop a concern for others. During early and middle adolescent years, there is usually more frequent conflict between teens and their parents. Often, this is because the youths are trying to assert their individuality, and are exercising their independence.

By late adolescence, adolescents would have developed a separate identity from their parents. They may move away from their peer groups and strive to achieve adult status and fortunately, the conflicts with parents may very well have declined.

Typically, they will become closer to their parents again. If they and their parents enjoyed a somewhat close, trusting and loving relationship prior to adolescence, then these same qualities are usually restored during late adolescence when conflict lessens. As they begin to enter more permanent relationships, they establish responsible behaviour, and their personal value systems mature.

Your role as a parent during their identity formation stage is to...

1. Lead by example. You are your child's first role model and you will be shocked by how much they have learnt from you, just by seeing and observing you. For them to build a healthy identity, model the type of person you want

them to be. (Remember, start with the end in mind.)

2. Teach them your family values and the word of God early. Ensure they have a proper understanding for them to internalize your teachings. Model whatever you are teaching them.

3. Share your growing up stories with them -- things you've done in the past that you wished you never did. Tell them about your achievements too.

4. Influence them by motivating them with encouraging words; avoid comparison and all attacks to their personality. Use positive discipline methods.

5. Do not sweat the small stuff. There are some identities that might be just a phase that you can overlook, like their hairstyles, or growing a beard. The moment you sweat the small stuff, it becomes a major issue. (I know of someone whose son dyed his hair, but now he has his hair in a normal haircut and colour.) In my home, any identity-seeking that requires a

permanent change is not acceptable. Let your children know what is acceptable and what you can't indulge.

6. Show them you care about them by empathizing with them and validating their emotions.

7. Expose them to opportunities where they can discover their latent potentials and talents.

8. When they have discovered their talents and intelligences, create avenues for them to express and develop these talents. (More details in Chapter 3.)

9. Get interested in their friends, invite them to your home to visit; invite them all out to the movies or any fun place where they will be relaxed.

10. Ensure you have an open channel of communication with your children; it will be easier to engage in an ongoing sexuality conversation with them.

11. You can also get your teenager a mentor who shares your values and worldviews.

42

CHAPTER 2

UNDERSTANDING THE BRAIN DEVELOPMENT OF ADOLESCENTS AND ITS IMPACTS ON THEIR BEHAVIOUR

This chapter is very important, because every parent needs to know how the brain of their adolescent develops and how it functions, to understand and connect with them better. Most of their behaviours are as a result of how their brain functions.

The brain development in humans starts before birth and continues until early adulthood. The brain is fully developed by the mid-twenties. This development starts from the back of the head to the front of the head; the prefrontal cortex is the last to develop.

The brain can be divided into four. Each part has its function through which it helps humans to adapt better to the living environment. I have highlighted the different parts and their functions below.

1. The spinal cord and the base of the brain that deliver messages to and from all parts of the body, and control what happens in the parts

that you don't have to consciously think about like the heart, lungs, and digestion.

2. The cerebellum that controls and coordinates movement and other brain processes.

3. The amygdala and hippocampus that control emotion and memory.

4. The cortex that connects up all the senses and thinking part, including the prefrontal cortex which is involved in fine judgement and control.

PICTURE OF THE ADOLESCENT BRAIN PARTS AND THEIR FUNCTIONS

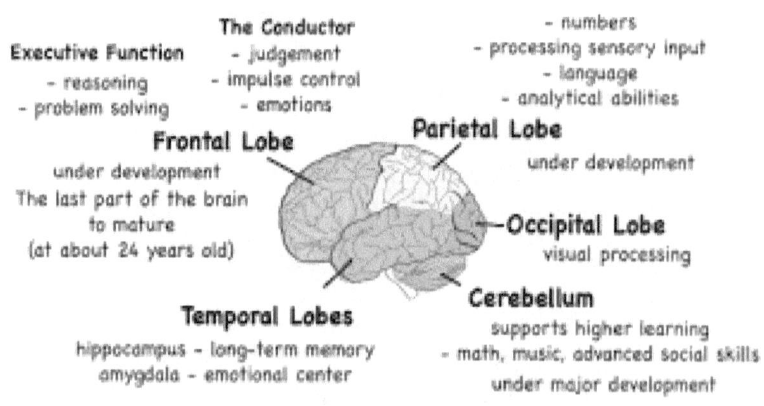

The prefrontal cortex is responsible for the following executive functions:

1. Complex decision making.

2. Planning skills (thinking and planning about the consequences of action).

3. Impulse control.

4. Emotional reactions and control.

5. Focused attention.

6) Prioritizing competing information received all at once.

7) The ability to ignore external distractions.

Adolescence is a time of significant growth and development inside the brain. The brain is being reshaped and rearranged; during this process, the prefrontal cortex is also still developing.

The main change is that unused connections in the thinking and processing part of your child's brain (called the grey matter) are 'pruned'. These are knowledge, skills or things your child learnt in the past but was not using consistently which might be forgotten, like playing an instrument or speaking a language. The pruning helps to create pathways for new activities. During this stage, other connections are strengthened. They can learn new skills and behaviour because the brain is malleable and neuroplastic. Neuroplasticity is the brain's way of becoming more efficient based on the 'use it or lose it' principle.

(In my younger years, I lived in Hamburg, Germany with my family and I could speak German fluently. Unfortunately, on moving to the United Kingdom where I lived for a few years, I had no one to speak the language with and of course, the skill fizzled out.) This pruning process begins in the back of the brain. The front part of the brain, the prefrontal cortex, is remodelled last. The prefrontal cortex is the decision-making part of the brain, responsible for your child's ability to plan and think about the consequences of actions, solve problems, and control impulses. Changes in this part continue into early adulthood.

Because the prefrontal cortex is still undergoing development, the teenagers might rely on a part of the brain called the amygdala to make decisions and solve problems, unlike adults who will use the prefrontal cortex to make decisions. The amygdala is associated with emotions, impulses, aggression and instinctive behaviour. Because of the amygdala, they do not think logically like adults, but emotionally.

Research has shown that during the adolescent years, your children use the emotional part of their brain(that is fully developed) more than the thinking brain (still developing) to make decisions due to the continued brain development. That's why they might behave impulsively and irrationally. There was a time my son jumped on a car and when asked, he said he was not thinking.

Your role during this stage is to be their emotions coach (more about this in Chapter 6) and to teach them to **ACT** before they act. **ACT is** an acronym for Apply Consequential Thinking. This process involves **pausing for about 6 seconds**, then assessing or evaluating their choices, envisaging how people will react, and imagining the upside and downside of their actions before taking the action.

The phrase 'look before you leap' applies here.

CHAPTER 3

UNDERSTANDING YOUR ADOLESCENT'S UNIQUENESS

'Teach your children that they're unique; that way, they won't feel pressured to be like everybody else.' — Cindy Cashman

Every child, including your adolescent, has a special and unique way that he or she responds to the environment, to love, and to learning. We are all products of nature and nurture. Nature is the factory-installed setting in everyone; the way we are wired to respond to our environment, to love, to learning and to people. Nurture is based on our individual experiences and the way we have been raised.

Every child has a factory-installed setting that can be altered, if not nurtured properly. Most times, we ignore this factory setting and just want to raise our children based on our past experiences or based on the way our parents raised us -- by default. To get the best out of your adolescents, you have to observe, recognise, identify and develop these inborn/innate traits in them. Your job as the parent is to identify this uniqueness and develop it by providing an enabling environment for your adolescent to thrive in.

For you to understand your adolescents, you have to know their innate traits. I will be using four different parameters to identify your child's uniqueness.

1)   The way he/she responds to the environment -- temperament/personality.

2)   The way he/she responds to love -- love language

3)   The way he/she responds to learning -- learning style.

4)   The special abilities or skills in him/her -- multiple intelligences.

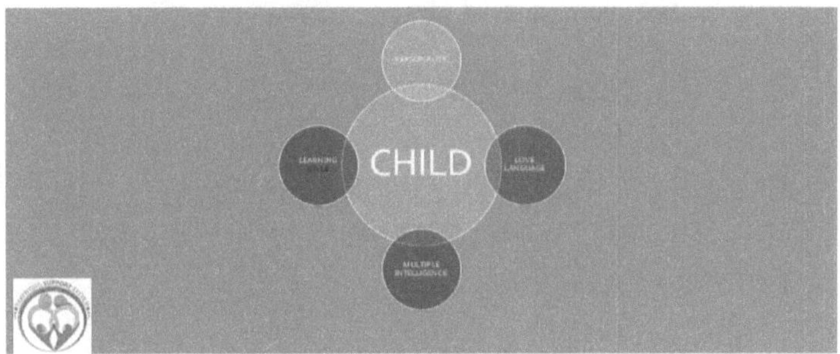

In my book, **Smart Parenting,** I wrote in detail about identifying your child's temperament and love language. I have summarised these in this book, but will discuss learning style and multiple intelligences in detail.

PERSONALITY TYPE

Personality type refers to the psychological classification of different types of individuals, while temperaments are the inborn traits your child uses in responding or reacting to the environment. There are different temperament and personality models, based on the assessment you would use. I will like to use the one formed by Hippocrates. The foundation for personality types was laid by Hippocrates; he identified four major personality types which others have developed into different types. For the benefit of this book and its readers, I will summarise these four personality types and their characteristics.

1)   CHOLERIC PERSONALITY TYPE

These are the adventurous, determined, outspoken, competitive, and strong-willed people (goal-oriented).

2)   SANGUINE PERSONALITY TYPE

These are the playful, sociable, talkative, lively and imaginative people (fun-oriented).

3)   MELANCHOLY PERSONALITY TYPE

These are detailed, orderly, pessimistic, reflective, reserved and very deep individuals.

4)   PHLEGMATIC PERSONALITY TYPE

These are thoughtful, controlled, adaptable, attentive, calm and diplomatic persons.

Based on the personality types I have highlighted, you will notice that all children are not the same. My three children all have three different personality types; I cannot relate with them all in the same way.

You will have to relate to each adolescent based on his/her personality type. For example, if your adolescent is choleric, they would love to do things their way and will be very assertive. If you, the parent, are also choleric, you would notice that you both are always at loggerheads.

The best way to relate with this personality type is to always give him/her options within set limits and boundaries.

Adolescents that are sanguine are playful and full of fun. As a parent, you will have to set appropriate limits and boundaries, and also ensure they have a daily schedule to put them in check and to manage their time effectively. My daughter is sanguine; she is very friendly and is the life of any place she finds herself. Due to this trait, she gets carried away with socializing while doing a task, so I have to set a timer for her to redirect her when I notice that she has lost track of time. I also give her a head start whenever we have to do a task together.

You have to understand your adolescent's personality for you to connect with him/her.

LOVE LANGUAGE

According to Dr.Gary Chapman, **'Knowing your child's love language makes a whole lot of difference in your relationship'.** Love is the foundation of any relationship. Everyone has a unique way of receiving and giving love. To raise your child without losing your cool, you need to know your child's love language. Love language is the way your child responds to love. We all have emotional needs and tanks that require to be filled. One of the major rules of parenting states that you need to love your child unconditionally. This can be achieved by understanding and knowing how your child responds to love, and loving the child the way he/she wants.

Gary has identified five love languages which I have stated below:

Tender Physical Touch: Expressing love by hugging, kisses, high fives, or a pat on the back.

Words of Affirmation: Using words of praise, love endearments, and encouragement to express love.

Quality Time: Giving your child undivided attention; being physically and emotionally available.

Gifts: A child sees the giving and receiving of gift as a powerful expression of love.

Acts of Service: This is when you do little things with your child to show you care for him/her.

These love languages can be used as a great tool in positive reinforcement of rules and discipline.

LOVE LANGUAGES

According to Vince Gowmon, 'Children learn and listen more willingly when they are met with love, kindness, empathy and patience. This is when their core need for connection or attachment is met'.

LEARNING STYLE

The way your child responds to learning is known as his/her learning style. Every child has a unique way of learning that every parent needs to help the child to discover. No two children are the same when it comes to learning. You can give two children the same material, but both of them will process the information differently.

This is because each child has a separate learning style. There are children whose strengths lie in reading and writing, while others learn more when they see pictorial representations of what they are learning. Some learn best by touching and feeling or participating in an activity related to what they are learning. Helping your child to know their learning style will bring ease to them when learning, and help them perform to their fullest potential.

Discovering how your child learns can help him/her develop strategies for studying more effectively. You should know that children have more than one learning style; it's important to identify their dominant learning strength. Once you know your children's learning styles, you can present information to them in a way that matches their styles, making it easier for them to learn. This also helps when giving your children instructions or tasks.

If you have been complaining about the poor performance of your child in his academics, (which might be because of a lack of understanding of what type of a learner he is) you might need to check different ways of helping him/her. The problem most of the time is not the lack of assimilation or understanding on the part of the child; rather, it is the style of teaching and learning that can prevent the child from having a result-oriented learning experience.

After going through this chapter, let your children also read it to help them know their predominant learning style – it will be to their advantage. Understanding what their predominant learning style is will allow them to exploit their own mind powers. Research has shown that students perform better on tests and in exams if they use study techniques tailored to their own personal styles of learning.

I have expatiate on the four different learning styles created by Kiwi Neil Flemming in his VARK model of learning below:

Visual

Auditory

Read & Write

Kinesthetic

1. Visual (Seeing)

When you see a child who is always with a picture, chart, graph or any visual material to use as an aid in learning, you have found a child whose learning style is visual. The name explains itself. Visual learners are those that learn best when they have an image or cue to help them process the information. They may also need to map out or write down their thoughts in order to really process what they are thinking.

Without a visual aid, visual learners can't enjoy their learning experience. Where a child is involved, this can frustrate his/her learning experience. If your child is a visual learner, he/she needs your support to provide visual material at home, to remove any form of frustration from his/her learning experience. Have you wondered how your child quickly remembers words and understands when he/she sees it in visual forms? It is because your child is a visual learner.

TIPS TO HELP YOUR ADOLESCENT

- Produce visual representations of material such as timelines, charts, outlines, pictures, etc.

- Use flashcards.

- Place emphasis on using texts and notes.

- They learn best when material is presented graphically.

- Incorporate creative visualization techniques for information retrieval.

2) Auditory

A child who is an auditory learner retains information best when it is presented through sound and speech. When you see a child who learns with the aid of sound, he or she doesn't need to struggle to have a result-oriented learning experience. As a parent, don't begin to take away sound systems from the house, as your child uses them to learn. I had this issue with my older son; whenever he was studying, he would have his earphones plugged into his ears and I will be like, 'How can you be learning and assimilating with this noise?' But he told me that he learns better with music in the background.

To others, it may be a distraction but for your child, it is not. What most parents see as not relevant to the learning experience of a child can be relevant when it is that child's learning style. Generally, a child who is an auditory learner always remembers what the teacher says and readily participates in class. For a child whose learning style is auditory, it is inclusive in the learning process for the child to seek audio learning methods which range from studying with voice recordings, to memorizing words by inventing short songs.

Some children prefer to learn with auditory learning aids like forming short songs, or with music playing in the background.

TIPS TO HELP YOUR ADOLESCENT

- Recite material out loud when studying/reading.

- Record class sessions. (Be sure to clear this with the instructor first.)

- Record him/her while he/she is reading notes and text.

- Create a study group for your child both at home and in school. An auditory learner thrives when he/she listens to others and learns from them.

- Review lectures aloud with a study buddy.

3. Read and Write (learning by reading and writing)

This learning style is a common category that most children fall into. It is in line with the conventional, school-taught study method of reading textbooks and writing notes. A child who loves to take notes in class and still helps his/her classmates to copy notes is not just doing it for fun; that is their learning style. Through writing and reading, they gather more information that ordinarily, they won't have.

Children whose learning style is reading and writing are good at taking notes in class even when others are saying the notes are much. They don't show signs of fatigue because as they write, information is being stored and processed in their brain. They study best by reading over these notes or copying them out. They enjoy reading. Sometimes you will find them in the library checking up books related to the class lectures, so they can get more understanding on the topic. This is my learning style.

Read-and-write learners are people who love to get details and explanations through reading more, despite what they were taught in class. They like to work by themselves in the quiet and make detailed notes of what they are studying: what concepts they are learning and points they are remembering. Children with this learning style are voracious readers. They are hungry for knowledge and don't get satisfied until they have gotten the explanation they need.

Learners like this need to be given detailed notes, explanations and essays with all the theories covering different perspectives. They always write out the various things they are learning, and write again until it becomes part of them. They make use of handouts and bullet points, and divide different parts to be learnt into categories and paragraphs.

TIPS TO HELP YOUR ADOLESCENT

1. Encourage your child to always have a notepad and pen to take notes when studying.

2. Rewriting of notes is the most efficient way to get those important facts drilled into his/her brain.

3. Let him/her study in a quiet room.

4. Turn diagrams and graphs into notes (words).

5. Studying in a library with lots of books is great.

Tactile/Kinesthetic

People who have this learning style learn best when incorporating the sense of touch and/or motion. They learn by touching and doing: dancing, acting, construction, or athletics.If your child is a **tactile learner**, he/she **learns best** by touching ,doing and physical activities. They understand and remember things through physical movement. He/she is a "hands-on" **learner** who prefers **to** touch, move, build, or draw whatever they learn.

Children who are tactile learners could be restless if they are not busy doing things.

They remember best what has been done, not what they have seen or talked about. They prefer direct involvement in what they are learning. They are distractible and find it difficult to pay attention to auditory or visual presentations. Rarely an avid reader, they may fidget frequently while handling a book.

Tips for Kinesthetic learner

- Hands on learning tools should be given. like a computer.

- write and rewrite data ot notes

- learn better by use of games and projects

- Pace while reading/studying.

- Take short breaks at intervals while studying

- Use dance, play or role play to reinforce learning..

- Encourage outdoor learning experiences

- Incorporate creative visualization techniques for information retrieval.

MULTIPLE INTELLIGENCES (M.I)

The mistake some parents make when it comes to the intelligence and ability of their children is that they focus only on the child's logical and linguistic abilities; (math and english) but there is more to your child than his/her ability to understand math and english. This has caused a lot of rebellion from adolescents and also, conflict between parents and adolescents. Your child has much more abilities and intelligence than you can ever imagine. If these abilities are identified, they will go a long way in helping the child become all he/she was created to be.

Your adolescent's success should not be based only on their ability to excel in mathematics and english language (these are just the foundations), but also on their ability to excel in their natural giftings/talents. If you have a child that is good in music, sports, cooking, fashion, etc. support him/her to become the best. The creative space is expanding, different careers are springing up daily. Content creators are coming up with wonderful ideas. Help your child to identify his/her uniqueness; harness and support him/her, and you will see a different adolescent emerge.

You bring out the best in your child when you are genuinely interested in his/her interests, and it can be a source of motivation.

Howard Gardner, a psychologist, in his book Multiple Intelligences has identified 8 other intelligences. Having more information about these intelligences will help you understand your child's strengths and abilities, which in turn will help with his/her future career choice. In his theory of multiple intelligences, Howard Gardner challenges the idea of a single IQ, where human beings have one central 'computer' where intelligence is housed. He says that there are multiple types of human intelligence, each representing different ways of processing information. I have highlighted them below.

- Verbal-linguistic intelligence refers to an individual's ability to analyse information and produce work that involves oral and written language such as speeches, books, and emails.

- Logical-mathematical intelligence describes the ability to develop equations and proofs, make calculations, and solve abstract problems.

- Visual-spatial intelligence allows people to comprehend maps and other types of graphical information.

- Musical intelligence enables individuals to produce and make meaning of different types of sounds.

- Naturalistic intelligence refers to the ability to identify and distinguish among different types of plants, animals, and weather formations found in the natural world.

- Bodily-kinesthetic intelligence entails using one's own body to create products or solve problems.

- Interpersonal intelligence reflects an ability to recognise and understand other people's moods, desires, motivations, and intentions.

- Intrapersonal intelligence refers to people's ability to recognise and assess those same characteristics within themselves.

Nature Smart
(Naturalist)

People Smart
(Interpersonal)

Number Smart
(Logical/Mathematical)

Picture Smart
(Spatial/Visual)

Self Smart
(Intrapersonal)

Body Smart
(Bodily-Kinesthetic)

Music Smart
(Musical)

Word Smart
(Linguistic)

The following guideline was developed by The Child Development Institute; you can use the questions below as guides to observe your adolescent so you can identify his/her multiple intelligences.

Bodily-Kinesthetic Intelligence

Does your child...

1. Excel in more than one sport?

2. Move various body parts when required to sit still for long periods of time?

3. Have the ability to mimic others' body movements?

4. Enjoy taking things apart and putting them back together?

5. Have a hard time keeping hands off objects?

6. Enjoy running, jumping, or other physical activities?

7. Show skill in activities that require fine motor coordination like origami, making paper airplanes, building models, finger-painting, clay, or knitting?

8. Use his/her body well to express himself/herself?

Interpersonal Intelligence

Does your child...

1. Enjoy socializing with friends?

2. Seems to be a natural leader?

3. Empathise easily with others, which leads to their giving advice to friends who come to them with problems?

4. Seems to be street smart?

5. Enjoy belonging to organizations?

6. Enjoy teaching other kids – either peers or younger ones?

7. Have two or more close friends?

8. Serve as a magnet for social activities with others?

Intrapersonal Intelligence

Does your child...

1. Show a sense or independence or a strong will?

2. Have a realistic sense of his/her abilities and weaknesses?

3. Do well when left alone to play or study?

4. 'March to the beat of a different drummer' in living and learning?

5. Have a hobby or interest he/she doesn't talk about much?

6. Have a good sense of self-direction?

7. Prefer working alone to working with others?

8. Accurately express how he/she is feeling?

9. Learn from failures and successes?

10. Have a good self-esteem?

Linguistic Intelligence

Does your child...

1. Write better than average for his/her age?

2. Enjoy telling stories and jokes?

3. Have a good memory for names, places, dates and other information?

4. Enjoy word games, either visually or auditorily?

5. Enjoy reading books?

6. Spell better than other children of the same age?

7. Appreciate rhymes, puns, tongue twisters?

8. Enjoy audio books without needing to see the book itself?

9. Enjoy hearing stories without seeing the book?

10. Have an excellent vocabulary for his/her age?

11. Communicate thoughts, feelings and ideas well?

Logical-Mathematical Intelligence

Does your child...

1. Demonstrate curiosity about how things work?

2. Have fun with numbers?

3. Enjoy math at school? Enjoy math and/or computer games?

4. Play and enjoy strategy games such as chess and checkers, brain teasers, or logic puzzles?

5.   Easily put things into categories?

6.   Like to do experiments either at school when assigned, or on her own?

7.   Show an interest in visiting natural history or discovery-type museums and exhibitions?

Musical Intelligence

Does your child...

1.   Tell you when he/she recognises that music is off-key?

2.   Easily remember song melodies and sing them?

3.   Have a pleasant singing voice, either alone or in a choir?

4.   Play a musical instrument?

5.   Speak or move in a rhythmical way?

6.   Hum or whistle to himself/herself?

7.   Tap on the tabletop or desktop while working?

8.   Show sensitivity to noises in the environment?

9. Respond emotionally to music he/she hears?

Naturalist Intelligence

Does your child...

1. Talk about favourite pets or preferred natural spots?

2. Enjoy nature preserves, the zoo, or natural history museums?

3. Show sensitivity to natural formations? (Note that in urban environments, this type of 'formation' can include cultural icons.)

4. Like to play in water?

5. Hang around the pet in school or at home?

6. Enjoy studying the environment, nature, plants and animals?

7. Speak out about animal rights and earth preservation?

8. Collect bugs, flowers, leaves, or other natural things to show to others?

Spatial Intelligence

Does your child…

1. Recall visual details in objects?

2. Have an easy time learning to read and understand maps and charts in books?

3. Daydream a lot?

4. Enjoy the visual arts?

5. Demonstrate ability in using art materials and creating drawings, sculptures, or other three-dimensional objects?

6. Enjoy visual presentations such as videos, television, and movies?

7. Get a lot of information from illustrations in the books he/she reads?

8. Scribble, doodle, or draw on all available surfaces?

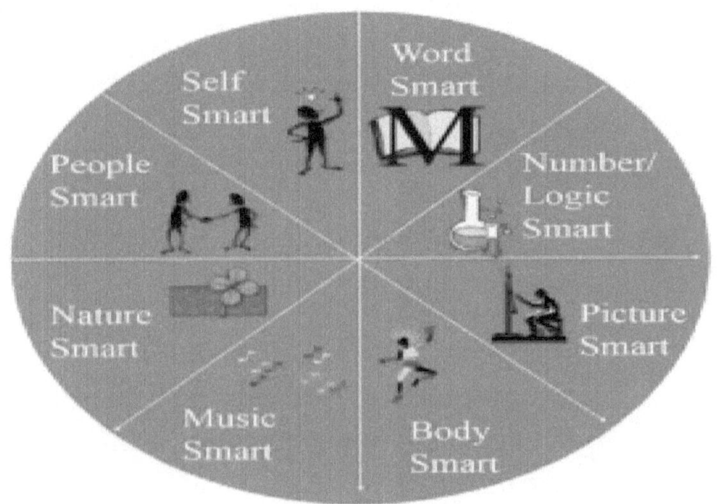

Role of parents in the development of multiple intelligences

Now that you know that every child has more than one intelligence, it will not be fair to focus or judge your child on his/her mathematical or linguistic abilities only. We are to develop and nurture their intelligences in at least 4 other intelligences to make them a success.

Imagine your child has a high level of logical intelligence, yet has no people skills (interpersonal intelligence); that would be a disaster for his/her career! That is why you need to help your child to identify his/her uniqueness and develop other latent potentials/intelligences to become the best version of himself/herself. The good news is that the brain is malleable; that means it can still learn new things for future use.

Below, I have highlighted how you can help your child to enhance these intelligences.

1. If you have an inquisitive adolescent, be always available to answer their questions; do not shut them down. Encourage them to seek more information.

2. Teach your child to enjoy reading books early from childhood (hardcopy or audiobooks).

3. Teach communication skills (verbal and non-verbal skills).

4. Encourage your adolescent to use mind mapping for critical thinking.

5. Teach your child to use the power of visualization. Develop his/her inner eyes.

6. Teach your child problem solving skills.

7. Practise mindfulness with your child; teach him/her to pay attention to little details in his/her environment.

8. Encourage your adolescent to engage in sporting activities.

9. Encourage mental math.

10. Develop his/her inner eyes.

11. Expose your child to different musical instruments.

Finally, remember you should not fix your child in a box. Celebrate the differences in each child. God has created each person as a masterpiece; please do not compare them.

CHAPTER 4

ADOLESCENTS AND THEIR SEXUALITY

Your child's sexuality is part of who they are. As he/she becomes an adolescent, he/she begins to experience changes in his/her body (which I have explained in Chapter 1) and begins to develop emotions due to hormones. The adolescent brain pours out adrenal stress hormones, sex hormones, and growth hormones. The production of testosterone increases 10 times in adolescent boys while in girls, the oestrogen hormones are produced, which causes the girl's body to mature, and prepares her for pregnancy.

Their hormone levels heighten, causing all sorts of emotions to go through them. Some of these emotions might be strange and confusing, as the adolescents start becoming aware of their sexuality. All this leads to their curiosity about sex and sexuality. This curiosity leads them to seek information from either their friends, or the internet (for children who do not have an open channel of communication with their parents). In the process of seeking knowledge, some end up acquiring pleasure via pornography. These pornographic materials are harmful to the brain of adolescents; they also affect their sexual o rientation. That is why you need to have the sexuality talk with your children earlier and continuously.

In my ebook, ***Talking About Sex,*** I have written about how to start the sex conversation with your adolescent. This sexuality conversation should have started earlier before adolescence.

Do you know that parents have a large influence on their adolescents' decisions about sex? Yet parents underestimate the impact they have on their children's sexual decisions. When some parents were asked, they actually assumed their children's friends had the most influence. Please, step into your role of influence and start this conversation with them.

For most parents and their children, the prospect of talking about sex and sexuality creates anxiety and apprehension; and this may lead to avoidance of discussions. Whenever I speak at any parents' forum in schools or churches about sexuality and I ask how many parents have started the sex talk with their children, always, more than half of the audience would say they have not started. When asked why, they say that they do not know what to say or how to start this conversation. This was one of the reasons I created a customised course for parents of adolescents, titled ***'Sex Ed for Parents of Adolescents: Starting the Sex Conversation'.***

The world has made sex mysterious and tempting, while some parents have presented it as dirty and sinful. That's why teens may want to experiment and test the waters. (Remember, their brains are wired towards excitement and rewards.) You are to demystify this by talking about it. **Sex is a gift from God to married couples for intimacy, fun, joy and procreation**. The earlier you start to talk about it with your children, the more comfortable they will become to speak to you about their concerns and fears. Use age appropriate teachings.

I am an advocate for sexuality education starting from home. You know the values you want to instil in your children; let your family and religious values be the standard for your children, and not what the world or the media is defining sex and sexuality to be. Speak to your children about sexual orientation based on your beliefs. Teach them about purity and not just virginity. Purity has to do with morality; it involves the body, the soul and the mind, while virginity has to do with the body.

Let your conversation on sex include:

Abstinence: This is the best form of protection. Let your child know that research has shown that it is not all teens that are involved in premarital sexual activities; so, they do not need to fall for peer pressure. Teach them to be the standard.

Consent: Teach your daughter that she has every right to say NO, and teach your male adolescent and young adult that any form of resistance or hesitation on the part of the lady means NO. They are to respect themselves and others.

Protection: Let them know that premarital sex leads mostly to heartbreaks, pregnancy, and sexually transmitted diseases (STD's). The best way to protect themselves from these is by abstaining from premarital sex.

During my classes on **Sex Ed for Parents of Adolescents**, I teach parents that they should practise or role-play different scenarios at home with their children and use those practices to teach their children how to respond to any scenario, so they are not caught unawares. Children who have not been taught about sexuality education when caught unawares, do not have enough options on how to respond. I remember when my daughter was younger.

I had taught her about appropriate and inappropriate touches and one of the things I told her was to always scream when she feels uncomfortable. We had practised this several times at home.

There was a particular day that someone tried to touch her in an inappropriate way. The way she screamed STOP IT drew a lot of attention and the man was so embarrassed that he ran off.

TIPS ON STARTING SEXUALITY EDUCATION WITH YOUR ADOLESCENT

1. Start when they are younger, so it will be an easier topic for conversation during adolescence. Use age appropriate teachings.

2. To have this conversation with your adolescent, you need to have built a trusting relationship where there is rapport and an open channel of communication.

3. Always look for teachable moments like when watching television/movies, or when there is breaking news about sexuality issues.

4. Use your questioning tool. Always start by asking open-ended questions. Your child's response will give you an idea of what to discuss with him/her.

5. You can also start when the child hits puberty.

6. Talk with them when you are both doing activities (fun activities, of course).

PORNOGRAPHY

Pornography is a high-risk habit that some adolescents are involved in. Parents should know that pornographic material can be accessed freely and easily -- it's just a click away. Unknown to these teenagers, exposure and viewing of pornographic materials may cause emotional, psychological, social and physiological disorders.

When having the sex conversation, always speak to them about the effects of pornography on them.

EFFECTS OF PORNOGRAPHY ON YOUR ADOLESCENT

The first thing you need to let your child know is that the first effect of pornography is that it leads to addiction. The effect of addiction to pornography on the brain is similar to the effect of drugs on the brain of a drug addict.

His brain chemistry is altered; the dopamine rush a drug addict experiences during a fix is the same as the rush one gets when addicted to pornography. When an adolescent watches pornography, he/she gets instant gratification by the rush of dopamine into his/her system; and since the brain is easily motivated by perceived rewards of pleasure, they crave for more.

There was a case that I handled a few years ago about a 9-year-old girl who was addicted to porn. During counselling, when asked how she got into it, she said while watching the tv at home after school, she saw two women kissing and she decided to search on her phone, only for the search engine to show different videos. Her curiosity led her to open and download the videos.

As parents, ensure your pre-teen's internet-enabled phone has parental control.

Apart from the risk of addiction, below are some other effects of pornography:

1. Sexual orientation is altered – LGBTQ.

2. Degree of body shame due to the unrealistic photoshopped sexual parts of porn stars.

3. The child's behaviour is affected; he or she becomes physically and verbally aggressive (like an addict).

4. Unhealthy sexual preference – fetish sexual desires.

5. Unrealistic sexual beliefs and values.

TRAP OF THE PORN INDUSTRY

Due to the addictive nature of pornographic material and the fact that the brains of children are malleable, the porn industry targets these children.

If you are observant when your children are watching cartoons on tabs or desktops, you will notice that all sorts of videos pop up; and out of curiosity, they might click on them and boom! they get introduced to porn.

ROLE OF PARENTS IN THE SEXUALITY EDUCATION OF ADOLESCENTS

1. Establish family values (belief systems).

2. Set family norms (spoken and unspoken rules).

3. Set appropriate boundaries and limits.

4. Filter and censor their media consumption -- what they listen to, watch, read and do on the internet.

5. Porn-proof your home and devices.

6. Protect them with parental control and guidance.

7. Develop their self-confidence, self-esteem and self-worth.

8. Constantly have positive talks with them.

CHAPTER 5

YOUR ADOLESCENT AND THE INTERNET

Caller: *Good afternoon, ma. You do not know me but I follow you on Instagram and I see what you are doing.*

Me: *Thank you for following me. How may I help you, ma?*

Caller: *I have a challenge but I do not know who to talk with. My child is addicted to his screen; he is always online chatting with people even late into the midnight. He is also into pornography. What can I do? How can you help me?*

I often get calls like this from parents who have caught their children with pornographic material on their devices. With the availability of and easy access to the internet, we now have children indulging in pornography and other unwholesome activities. The internet is a useful tool that our children can use to their advantage. It can bring loads of opportunities to them. They can acquire new skills on it (my son learnt to cut his hair on the internet), it helps them academically and teaches them more about countries they have not been to, or people they have never met.

The internet has brought the world closer and made it a global village.

However, **there are also dangers that the unsupervised usage of the internet can bring.** As a parent, you are to be deliberate in raising your child, and intentional about carrying out your role. Using the internet has its advantages and disadvantages. Children of this generation are known as the digital natives, while we are known as the digital migrants because we were from a pre-digital age and had to learn more about the internet. But these children were born into the computer, internet and social media era where all they need to do to know more about the internet is simply to hold the device, and they are good to go. Our role is to teach them healthy usage of the internet.

ADVANTAGES OF THE INTERNET FOR CHILDREN

Academics: It helps with their homework, research, school communication, and online reading.

Skills development: They can learn new skills like coding, cooking, communication, etiquette, music, etc.

Recreational activities: Recreational activities like games, workout, tips for sports can also be gotten online.

Encourage your children to make the best use of their time online.

DISADVANTAGES OF UNSUPERVISED USAGE OF THE INTERNET

- Inappropriate content (pornography).

- Cyberbully

- Sexual and crime predators.

- Cyber fraud

- Screen addiction

How do you protect your child?

1)   The first thing to do as a parent is to teach yourself more about the internet and its usage, then you educate your children about its safe usage. Teach them responsible online behaviour: this is called **netiquette.**

- Rule 1: Everyone online is human; treat them with respect.

- Rule 2: Adhere to the same standards of behaviour online that you follow in real life.

- Rule 3: Know where you are in cyberspace.

- Rule 4: Respect other people's time and bandwidth.

- Rule 5: Share true information, not fake or inappropriate information.

2)   Give them basic guidelines and healthy boundaries, talk to them about their digital footprints -- anything they post online stays online. Their digital footprints might be checked when they are seeking admission or employment in the future.

3)   Create family rules like: do not trade nude pictures; know the type of pictures to post; do not share passwords or personal information; respect other people online. Teach your child to keep personal information private online.

YAPPY is a useful acronym to remind children of some of the personal information they should not share on public online spaces (blogs, forums, social media, etc.). YAPPY stands for **Y**our full name, **A**ddress, **P**hone number, **P**asswords, **Y**our plans and birthday.

Speak to your child about instant messaging and chat rooms; he/she should avoid talking to strangers online. The same way they are wary of physical strangers, they should be wary of online strangers.

4) Teach them to adhere to family rules for screen time like not using phones during meal times, and having a cut-off time for internet usage.

5) If you are to give a child an internet-enabled device (mobile or stationary), you are to protect him/her by supervising his/her internet usage and installing online protection tools/software on all devices (mobile and gaming devices). This is to protect or control their access to inappropriate and unhealthy content and also, to block access to certain sites.

Let them know that it's not everything online that is true; let them verify the source of the information.

Monitor, regulate and track the online activities of your teenagers by following all their social media handles. (But please do not comment, unless you want to be blocked and unfriended.) Most teenagers have two social media accounts.

As your children get older, your control over their internet usage decreases. You will only be able to influence them; that's why you need to have done a proper job in educating them when they were younger. There are countless virtual sites you need to be aware of, and teach them to be smart users of.

Encourage your children to have screen off days where they can still learn to have fun without their mobile devices or their screens. Encourage board games, outdoor activities like taking a nature walk, playing sports, or aerobic exercise.

The internet is here to stay. Let's prepare and teach our children to be smart users by knowing about its advantages and disadvantages.

Screen Addiction

What is addiction? Addiction is dependency, weakness, craving, compulsion, fixation or enslavement on an activity or substance. Addiction is the psychological and physical inability to stop an activity, drugs, or substance. Screen addiction is a new reality that we need to put in check. My son said that because it is not being stigmatized and probably because it has not been categorized as a disorder, people still do not believe that they have a problem with their screen usage. However, we spend too much time on technology, and it is affecting our daily functions.

Screen addiction is not just about gaming, but has to do with every form of technology: your tv, laptop, phones. It is not just the time you spend with your devices, but how you use them.

There are questions that you have to answer with your child. How does the use of your devices affect other areas of your life? Do you find yourself not accomplishing set goals? Do you turn to your phone for comfort when you are bored, or to escape any situation?

Signs of Screen Addiction

1)   If it affects one's daily activities: bed time, meal time, everyday communication and school work.

2)   Spending more time with virtual friends instead of real people.

3)   Screen time gives one great joy every day.

4)   It's a cause of major conflicts.

5)   One spends more and more time online.

6)   The quality of one's work suffers.

UNPLUGGING YOUR TEENS FROM THEIR SCREENS

How do you help your teen to unplug from his/her screens? Below are a few steps:

1. Be a good role model when it comes to phone/devices usage.

2. Create rules surrounding the use of devices in the home.

3. Create a device-free zone in your home.

4. Encourage your child to get off their phones for a specified period daily, or have a screen-free day.

5. Get your child interested in sport activities like football, basketball, etc.

6. Let them be interested in other activities like board games, painting, singing, music writing, etc.

CHAPTER 6

EMOTIONAL AND MENTAL WELLBEING

I have divided this chapter into three. I will be talking about how you can manage your emotions as a parent, how you can help your child become emotionally intelligent, and how to protect your child's mental well being.

The secret to raising your child without losing your cool is to understand and manage the emotions in you. Parenting starts with you. The greatest challenge that most parents have is that of managing their own emotions.

I have heard parents blaming their children for the way they, the parents, act. You have to own your emotions. Our emotions are real, valid and neutral, but what we do with them determines if they are empowering or not.

When I became a mother, I saw another side of myself that I never knew existed. I was a yelling mummy; I just couldn't control my emotions. Thankfully, I got help. So, I understand when clients whom I coach in my *No Yelling Course* explain how they feel when their children ignore their instructions, or are outrightly disobedient.

When you feel flustered, angry or frustrated, the emotions are valid, but how you respond to these emotions determines if they can be helpful or hurtful. How you react to your emotions greatly affects your children's ability to self-regulate, their self-control and their general emotional wellness, because you are their first role model.

HOW DO YOU MANAGE YOUR EMOTIONS AS A PARENT?

The first step in managing your emotions is self-awareness. It starts with you becoming aware of your emotions (what you are feeling) and understanding those emotions. Identifying your triggers (what is making you feel that way) is also important. Relevant questions: Why do I get upset each time I get back from work?

Why do I feel frustrated when I am helping my son with his homework? Why do I yell every morning when I am getting ready for work? These are questions you need to ask and answer.

The best way to identify your trigger is to observe yourself and your body cues (signs that let you know that you are worked up) for a number of days, and use a journal to record your findings. In my book, **Parenting Journal**, I have an emotion tracker that you can use to track the different emotions you feel daily, and also identify your triggers and body cues.

The next step in managing your emotions is self-regulation. After becoming aware of your triggers, you have to regulate yourself so you start responding, and not reacting. Self-regulation is the ability to consciously use healthy strategies to control your emotions. The essence of self-regulating is to turn your natural reaction of yelling/anger to an empowering and deliberate response.

The act of pausing before acting is very important. Pause for a few seconds before you react to any triggering event, then use those few seconds to take a deep breath, **apply consequential thinking**, reappraise and reinterpret the situation.

In the online **No Yelling Course** I created for parents, we have an exercise in one of the modules that requires parents to look for alternatives to yelling. What other things can you do when you find yourself in a situation where you might lose your cool, especially with your children? This is where applied consequential thinking takes place. Use the few seconds or minutes of pausing to think through your next line of action. Think of the consequences of your actions, the upside and downside.

Below, I have stated a few alternatives to yelling (an excerpt from our *No Yelling Guide*).

1. Stop what you are doing. Take a few deep breaths.

2. Count from 1-10.

3. Walk away.

4. Talk it out with your spouse or an accountability partner.

5. Take a time out/off as a parent.

6. Listen to music.

7. Drink water.

Now that you know how to control your emotions, you have to help your adolescent to manage their emotions and challenges by being their emotions coach.

In the previous chapters, I discussed the changes in adolescents that lead to the secretion of hormones that affect their emotions. It's a fact that adolescents are known for their mood swings. One moment, they are all happy, talkative and friendly; the next moment, you notice that they are moody, not wanting to talk to you. So, what can you do as a parent that wants to connect? How can you help them?

Like I stated earlier, all emotions are valid, especially those of your adolescent. You have to validate the emotions going through them. For example, your child comes home from school one day upset and cranky. You know something has happened to them. It's not the time to say, 'Man up, be a big boy', but a time to listen to them when they want to talk about what they are feeling.

It might be due to a test, or friends did something upsetting. Acknowledge how they feel, and ask what they would want to do. Because they use more of their emotional brain than the logical, executive brain function, you have to coach them to manage their emotions so they can act/behave appropriately.

If your child has a very high IQ but is not able to manage his/her emotions, the rate of his/her success and progress will be limited.

The book of Proverbs 16:32 (ISV) states that whoever controls his temper is better than a warrior, and anyone who has control of his spirit is better than someone who captures a city. It is very important that we teach our children how to manage their emotions.

You have to help your adolescent to acquire emotional intelligence. A person who has a high emotional intelligence quotient is someone who is smart with his/her emotions.

Emotional intelligence is the ability to be aware of and manage your emotions, and the ability to understand the emotions in others. Adolescents with high emotional intelligence are able to avoid impulsive outbursts and behaviours; they perform better at school. The ones who are not able to manage their emotions are prone to mental health disorders like anxiety and depression.

Remember, you are the adult -- you need to remain calm. Keep your cool when they have their emotional outbursts so you can help them process their big emotions; for example, when they have lost a game, when their friends disappoint them, or when they did not do well in an exam, etc. I remember when my son had an emotional outburst during a match in which he felt his team was being cheated by the referee. I had to walk him through the process of managing his emotions.

STEPS IN MAKING YOUR CHILD EMOTIONALLY INTELLIGENT

1. Teach your children to process how they feel, and not to suppress their emotions. Let them be in tune with their emotions.

2. Teach them to identify their body cues. These are indicators that let us know more about our emotions. For example, when I am getting upset, my voice quivers and my hands begin to shake.

3. Teach them to identify their triggers, e.g. when a friend makes fun of them.

4. Teach them how to self-regulate by taking deep breaths, walking away from the triggering event, counting from 1-10, etc.

5. Teach them alternative ways to release their pent-up emotions like writing in a journal, doing physical exercise like running, playing basketball, skipping, or any other form of sport. This will replace the urge of fighting or being aggressive to other people. Exercising releases some hormones called endorphins which are natural mood boosters. When teens engage in exercise, it gives them a sense of accomplishment and boosts their self-confidence.

6. Meditation: This teaches them to be focused on the now and the present, and stops their mind from wandering.

Getting your adolescent engaged in any form of sport is a good way for them to release their pent-up energy and emotions. Sports with rules and regulations also help to instil discipline.

MENTAL HEALTH OF ADOLESCENTS

According to the World Health Organization, 10-20% of children and adolescents experience mental disorders. Half of all mental illnesses begin by the age of 14, and three-quarters by mid-twenties. Poor mental health can have negative effects on the wider health and development of adolescents, and is associated with several health and social outcomes such as alcohol, tobacco, and illicit substances use, adolescent pregnancies, school dropouts, and delinquent behaviours.

During my training in mental health disorder, it was discussed that most children who had undergone certain adverse experiences while growing up are prone to mental disorders in their adult life. Such adverse experiences include:

1. Neglect

2. Physical abuse

3. Sexual abuse

4. Emotional abuse

5. Witness violence/abuse

Mental disorders such as conduct disorders, anxiety, depression and eating disorders as well as other risk behaviours including those that relate to sexual behaviour, substance abuse, and violent behaviour are found in adolescents as young as 14.

I want you to know that the emotional wellbeing of children is just as important as their physical health. Good mental health allows children and young people to develop the resilience to cope with whatever life throws at them, and grow into well-rounded, healthy adults.

There is a growing consensus that healthy development during childhood and adolescence contributes to good mental health, and can prevent mental health problems.

Other factors are also important, including:

- feeling loved, trusted, understood, valued and safe.

- being interested in life and having opportunities to enjoy themselves.

- being hopeful and optimistic.

- being able to learn, and having opportunities to succeed.

- accepting who they are and recognising what they are good at.

- having a sense of belonging in their family, school and community.

- feeling they have some control over their own life.

- having the strength to cope when something is wrong (resilience), and the ability to solve problems.

Teenagers often experience emotional turmoil as their minds and bodies develop. An important part of growing up is working out and accepting who they are. Some young people find it hard to make this transition to adulthood, and may experiment with alcohol, drugs, or other substances that can affect mental health.

Below are some challenges that teenagers experience while growing up, that may lead to mental health breakdown:

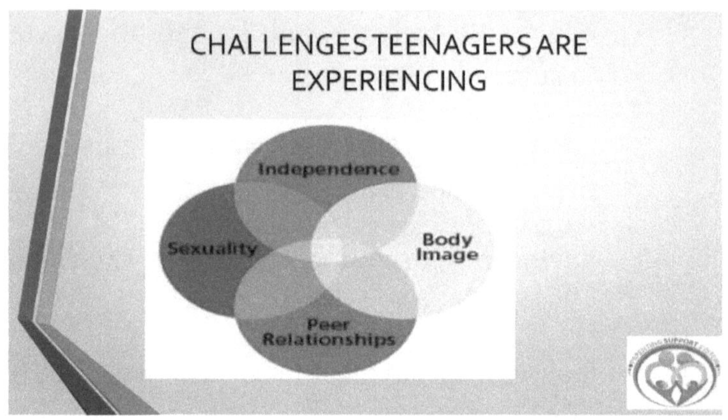

- Independence from parents
- Body image
- Peer pressure
- Sexuality
- Managing emotions

The Mental Health Organization of the UK has highlighted some mental health problems that can affect children and young people. Below is the list:

1. Depression affects more children and young people today than in the last few decades, but it is still more common in adults. Teenagers are more likely to experience depression than young children.

2. Self-harm is a very common problem among young people. Some people find that it helps them manage intense emotional pain, if they harm themselves through cutting or burning, for example. They may not wish to take their own life, however. (I had a client whose child was cutting herself. By the time we counselled and spoke to her, we found out that she had been emotionally and verbally abused by her cousin who was staying with her family.)

3. Generalised anxiety disorder (GAD) can cause young people to become extremely worried. Very young children or children starting or changing school may have separation anxiety.

4. Post-traumatic stress disorder (PTSD) can follow physical or sexual abuse: witnessing something extremely frightening or traumatising, being the victim of violence or severe bullying, or surviving a disaster.

5. Children who are consistently overactive (hyperactive), who behave impulsively and have difficulty paying attention may have attention deficit hyperactivity disorder (ADHD). Many

more boys than girls are affected, but the cause of ADHD isn't fully understood.

6.   Eating disorders usually start in the teenage years and are more common in girls than boys. The number of young people who develop an eating disorder is small, but eating disorders such as anorexia nervosa and bulimia nervosa can have serious consequences for their physical health and development.

If they have a warm, open relationship with their parents, children will usually feel free to tell them if they are troubled. **One of the most important ways parents can help is to listen to them and take their feelings seriously**. They may want a hug; they may want you to help them change something, or they may want practical help.

Children and young people's negative feelings usually pass. However, it's a good idea to get professional help if your child is distressed for a long time: if their negative feelings are stopping them from getting on with their lives, if their distress is disrupting family life, or if they are repeatedly behaving in ways you would not expect at their age.

CHAPTER 7

EFFECTIVE COMMUNICATION

'The most important thing in communication is hearing what isn't said.'

– Peter F. Drucker

'Effective communication begins with listening.'

--Robert Gately

Effective communication is the key to any relationship, including your relationship with your adolescent. Communication is not just the words you speak to your children, but also the way (tone and tact) you speak to them. It is a two-way process of transferring information from one person to another.

I have coached parents who have said it's difficult talking with their teenagers: it's either the teenagers are not listening, or they are just not responding. Every parent wants to have a great relationship with their children. The children too want to be able to speak with their parents when they have things bothering them. So, why is there a barrier in communication between parents and their adolescents?

The first thing you need to know about the process of communication between you and your children is that it evolves. The way you spoke to your child as a baby will be different from the way you will talk with your teenager. It will no longer be that of the dictator or issuing of commands; now, you have to talk with

consideration, avoid criticism and lectures. You have to use more of a conversational tone that is respectful, kind, and of course, be more patient with them.

In Chapter One, I spoke about the cognitive development of your adolescent, how he/she now starts thinking abstractly so that when you issue your instructions or commands, the next thing you will hear is 'why'.

When they say this, it is not them being rude, but them wanting more information or wanting you to clarify what you are saying. They will begin to assert themselves and form their own opinion about things. It's best not to give a narrow-minded this-is-how-it-is kind of opinion. It's advisable that you have an open-minded view when speaking with them, explaining things in detail, asking questions, and encouraging shared reflection.

The complaint of most teenagers is that they are not being heard or understood by their parents. Some say their parents are not available for them to speak with. There was a time when my younger son said he felt he was neither being heard nor understood. We had to be deliberate about talking and listening to him. We changed our communication style to be more effective. My husband dedicated a special one-on-one time for him.

So, how can we speak with our adolescents? How can we get them to listen to us? How can we get them to respond to us? Below are a few tips on effective communication with your adolescents:

EFFECTIVE COMMUNICATION TIPS FOR PARENTS

1. To get your adolescent to start talking with you, you have to build trust and rapport. Trust is the bedrock of any relationship and also an essential element in parenting. When your child trusts you, they know you have their best

> interest in mind; it will be easier for them to speak with you.

2.   Listening is a great tool in communication. It involves active participation where you pay attention to the verbal and non-verbal expression of your child. You do more listening than talking. You will realize that it is far more rewarding; it becomes easier for them to open up to you. This way, you get to know and understand their feelings, which is crucial as it provides pointers to what they are thinking, and where they need more support.

3.   Have an open communication channel where your child will feel free to tell you anything without you being judgemental or critical.

4.   Always give them a fair hearing; let them air their opinion and say what they have to say without you shutting them down. Talking to them without trying to impose your own ideas is another way to foster good communication.

5.   Be genuinely interested, and also show that you are interested in what they are saying. You can paraphrase (summarise) what you have heard.

6.   Give your full attention when interacting with them.

7.   Avoid giving your unsolicited advice. All they might need is just a listening ear.

8.   It is important to try to always be honest about what you think, say, and feel. This also means keeping the promises and commitments you make. This is how you build trust. Avoid sarcastic comments.

9.   Give them clear instructions that they can understand, and always ask if they understood what you said. Let them paraphrase what they heard.

10.   Include them in some decision-making processes in the home.

BARRIERS TO EFFECTIVE COMMUNICATION

- Interruptions and distractions. Not giving your child your full attention can make it seem like you are not interested in what they are saying.

- Jumping in with advice, rather than listening to what your child has to say.

- Judging what they have to say and not validating their point of view.

- Interrogating your child by firing questions at them.

- Using past discussions with you against them.

- Being quick to fix their issues.

When parents communicate effectively with their children, the children begin to feel that they are heard and understood by their parents, which is a boost to their self-esteem. On the other hand, communication between parents and children that is ineffective or negative can lead children to believe that they are unimportant, unheard, or misunderstood. Such children may also come to see their parents as unhelpful and untrustworthy.

The way you speak with your child determines their response or reaction towards you. Teach them to be respectful in the way they speak, by being respectful when speaking with them.

IMPORTANT CONVERSATIONS PARENTS SHOULD HAVE WITH THEIR ADOLESCENTS

I have stated how to start having effective communication with our children. Now, I will be discussing some conversations we should have with our children on a continuous basis.

FAITH (GOD & CHURCH):

Studies have shown that by the age of 13, children will have developed a belief system about their faith. Most children that will leave their faith have already decided to do so by this age; they are just waiting for their independence (age 18). You need to constantly speak with your child about your God and your faith. It is not just talking about your faith, but also living it. One of the reasons children leave their faith is the hypocrisy of their parents. Make it fun for them. Teach them that their faith is about them having a relationship with God, and not the religion.

SEX & RELATIONSHIPS:

In the chapter about your adolescent and his sexuality, I wrote that the sex conversation should be ongoing. This is to guide your child during his/her mid adolescence years. They will be interested in the opposite sex and may want to start dating or being in a relationship. Talk to them about premarital sex, abstinence, consent and protection. You know you cannot control them, but you can guide and influence them to do what is right by teaching your values early. Speak to them about respecting others -- being fair.

FUTURE ASPIRATIONS:

Speaking to your child about his future is important; it gives them a form of motivation to achieve more. Ask questions on how they would want to change the world. Speak to them about the university, about skills they would need to become the best in their chosen career path. Look at the natural skills they have and develop them. (My older son loves business and computers, so we are grooming him in a career path in line with his interest). Help them dream big; let them know you believe in them.

FINANCES:

This is another topic I feel parents should discuss with their children. Let them know the monetary value of what they have, of what you buy for them.

This makes them appreciate it better. Let them know how to operate an account, budget, and how to negotiate.

ALCOHOL AND DRUGS:

We need to speak to our adolescents about the effects of alcohol and drug usage on them. Drugs and alcohol have a greater effect on teens than on adults. The signs of addiction can be difficult to understand, and many adolescents do not realise the long-term damage that drugs have on their bodies because the short-term side effects fade. Adolescents are prone to be addicted to these substances because of the way their brains are developing, and the release of dopamine into their brains.

When my son became a teenager, I enrolled him for a mental health and substance abuse course because he was going for a leadership training, and the topic he was to discuss was on mental health. He was taught about the way people get addicted and the effect of substance abuse on the brain, their behaviour, and even their future.

One thing that your children need to know is that no one knows if it is the first drink, drag or sniff of these substances that can get them addicted. When they get addicted to substances, it slows down their brain development and they are prone to mental health disorder.

I have just written about a few conversations you need to have with your children. These conversations are to put them in check and for you to guide them. Kindly note that these topics should be conversations, and not lectures or sermons.

CHAPTER 8

POSITIVE DISCIPLINE AND ADOLESCENTS

Discipline is one of the major issues that parents have with their adolescents. In my coaching practice, I have heard parents complaining that their adolescents are difficult to manage or control. I have also heard parents saying that their children do not obey their rules, or follow instructions. They have asked how they can discipline their children to follow their instructions. Another issue that parents are a bit worried about is how to balance love with discipline.

Let me start by saying that discipline is not the same as punishment. This is a major mistake a lot of parents make. I will give brief details on the difference between the two. Discipline has to do with teaching, guiding and leading. It means to develop behaviour by instruction and practice; it also means to teach self-control. The word discipline comes from Latin *disciplina* (teaching, learning or instruction), and *discipulus* (disciple, pupil). To teach is to show and explain how to do something. It focuses on imparting desirable *future* behaviour.

Discipline is used by parents to teach about their expectations, guidelines, family and community rules, or principles. When it comes to correcting your adolescent's misbehaviour, discipline will teach them how to make better choices in the future.

Punishment focuses on past misbehaviour, and offers little or nothing to help a child behave better in the future. It inflicts suffering on children for *past* behaviour. Punishment is not just philosophically bad; it is harmful to the brain.

Punishment instils a penalty for a child's offence. It is about making a child 'pay' for his/her mistakes. Sometimes, the desire to inflict punishment stems from a parent's feelings of frustration and anger, but never love. Punishment is about controlling a child, rather than teaching him/her how to control himself/herself. And most often, it alters the child's self-image.

EFFECTS OF PUNISHMENT (NEGATIVE DISCIPLINE)

1. Breakdown of relationship.

2. Rebellion

3. Leads to aggression in children.

4. Affects the brain development of the child.

5. Child develops antisocial and destructive behaviour.

Now that we know the difference between discipline and punishment, I will highlight how you can use positive discipline to teach, guide and lead your adolescent.

Positive discipline focuses on you being firm, fair, friendly (kind) and respectful. The ultimate goal of positive discipline is to help your adolescent develop self-discipline to manage himself/herself and live independently.

TIPS ON POSITIVE DISCIPLINE

1. Have an open channel of communication. You should have built a trusting, warm relationship with your child.

2. Set clear rules and expectations with your child, that he/she should have agreed on.

3. Use natural and logical consequences instead of punishment.

4. Be consistent and follow through with consequences.

5. Separate your child's misbehaviour from their personality. Most times, we treat them based on a misbehaviour. Please note that it is not who they are.

6. Always use solution-oriented discipline. This will teach your child to be a problem solver.

7. Reappraise your expectation of your children. Your expectations might be unrealistic.

Positive discipline

Positive discipline can be divided into positive reinforcement and negative reinforcement. Positive reinforcement is when you use a positive motivation to reward a desirable behaviour. The benefit of using this is to encourage the repetition of the desirable behaviour.

Negative reinforcement is when you use a negative stimulus to discourage an undesirable behaviour. Examples are grounding, withholding privileges and timeout. For this discipline to be effective, you need to know

your children and their uniqueness. For example, a child who loves his/her personal space will not feel the effect of grounding or timeout. Likewise, a child whose love language is not words of affirmation may not greatly appreciate being rewarded with praises or compliments.

Remove electronics. From smartphones to laptops, screen time is important to most teenagers. Restricting your teen's phone privileges can be an effective consequence. Just make sure it is time-limited. Usually, 24 hours is long enough to send a clear message to them.

Take away time with friends. If your teen's misbehaviour involves friends, take away his/her right to see pals for a while. Ground them for a few days or cancel their special weekend plans. A break from his/her buddies may remind him/her to make a better choice next time.

Tighten the rules. If your teen violates the rules, they may be showing you they cannot handle the freedom you are giving them. Tighten the rules by giving them an earlier curfew, or by reducing the amount of time they spend using their electronics.

•

Have your teen perform an act of restitution. If your teenager's behaviour hurts someone else, create a plan to make amends. Fixing something they broke or doing an extra chore for someone may help repair the relationship and remind them to accept responsibility for their behaviour.

•

Allow your teen to face natural consequences. Natural consequences can be the best teachers in certain situations. But it is important to make sure the natural consequences will really teach your teen a life lesson. If so, back off and let them face the consequences for their choices.

•

Provide logical consequences. If your teen breaks something, make them pay to fix it. Or if they are irresponsible with the car, take away their driving privileges. Create consequences that are directly tied to the poor choices they made.

•

Assign extra responsibilities. Take away their privileges until they complete extra chores or perform certain tasks. When they show you that they can be responsible, they can earn their privileges back.

Discipline with teenagers is complicated. They are at an age where it is important to give them more freedom and responsibility, but many parents feel like they have few tools at their disposal to hold teens accountable.

When parents strike the right balance of love with discipline, liberties with limitations and independence with responsibility, adolescents feel secure, valued, and loved. This is because adolescents feel secure when they know what is expected of them and have a clear understanding of the rules, boundaries and limitations, and the consequences for crossing the line.

They also feel secure knowing they can make mistakes without losing the love and care of their parents. They feel valued when parents set high but achievable standards for them. Furthermore, adolescents feel loved and valued when their parents express confidence in their abilities to make wise decisions and healthy choices, without allowing them to stray too far from the right path.

CHAPTER 9

EQUIP YOUR ADOLESCENT WITH LIFE SKILLS FOR SUCCESS

Congratulations! Your child has gained admission into an Ivy League school in another country and he would be leaving home in a few weeks. *Yaaay!* But wait a minute, have you prepared him for life outside your home? Have you

equipped him with the basic life skills to live an independent life?

This chapter is about the last stage of adolescence when your child will be preparing to leave home for independent living. Like I stated in the introduction, you need to equip your child with skills, values and characters that will prepare him/her for adulthood.

The last stage of adolescence is between the ages of 17-21. This is the stage that your child becomes physically mature, starts thinking about the future, and now understands how his/her choices and decisions affect his/her future.

The prefrontal cortex becomes fully developed by early adulthood. Your child is not influenced by his/her peers anymore, but starts making informed decisions. He/she understands right from wrong, knowing what is ethically and morally right.

Formal education gives your child the knowledge they need about different subjects and about their career, but it does not necessarily equip them with essential life skills. Your role is to teach them life skills to make this transition easy.

Life skills have been defined by the World Health Organization (WHO) as the abilities for adaptive and positive behaviour that enable individuals to deal effectively with the demands and challenges of everyday life. 'Adaptive' means that a person is flexible in their approach, and is able to adjust in different circumstances.

'Positive behaviour' implies that a person is forward-looking and even in difficult situations, can find a ray of hope and opportunities to find solutions.

Life skills enable individuals to translate knowledge, attitudes and values into actual abilities, i.e. what to do and how to do it. Life skills are abilities that enable individuals to behave in healthy ways, given the desire, the scope and the opportunity to do so.

ESSENTIAL LIFE SKILLS

1. Problem-solving skills

These skills will empower your adolescent to look at a problem objectively with the different, available options for solutions, and would help them come to a solution after weighing the pros and cons of the different options available. The first step to problem-solving is identifying the problem. When they have a problem, find out exactly what is bothering them and why it is a problem. Help them narrow down their problem by asking open-ended questions. Teach your children to face problems rather than run away from them. When your teen comes to you asking for advice, try not to jump in and resolve the problem for them. Ask them what they think they should do and help them work through possible options.

This is one skill we encourage in my home. Whenever there is a problem, we ask the children to all come up with their solutions, which we then fine-tune for them.

2.   Communication and negotiation skills

This is the ability to express ourselves both verbally and non-verbally, in ways that are appropriate to our cultures and situations. This means being able to express opinions and desires, but also needs and fears. And it may mean being able to seek advice and help in a time of need. We have an open channel of communication in our home; we encourage the children to speak up, we also have them take public speaking seriously. (I remember a time I took the children for a Toastmaster meeting; this was to expose them to public speaking.) Your child should be able to express his/her opinion without being afraid. For their negotiation skill, I encourage you to send them to the local market to buy stuff; this is to expose them to bargaining.

3.   Critical thinking skills

Critical thinking is the ability to analyse information and experiences in an objective manner. It can contribute in helping the adolescent to recognise and assess the factors that influence attitudes and behaviour such as values, peer pressure and the media. We ask our own kids to analyse issues in the news and come up with ideas and solutions.

4.   Creativity/creative thinking

This is a novel way of seeing or doing things that contributes to both decision-making and problem-solving by enabling us to explore the available alternatives and various consequences of our actions or non-action. It helps us to look beyond our direct experience. And even if no problem is identified, or no decision is to be made, creative thinking can help us to respond adaptively and with flexibility to the situations of our daily lives.

5.   **Coping with emotions (emotional intelligence)**

This refers to being able to recognise emotions within ourselves and others, being aware of how emotions influence behaviour, and being able to respond to them appropriately. An important aspect of this skill is learning to manage intense emotions like anger or sadness, which can have negative effects on our health, if we do not respond appropriately.

6.   **Empathy** is the ability to imagine what life is like for another person, even in a situation that we may not be familiar with. It is putting yourself in another person's shoes.

7.   Money and budgeting skills

Make sure your child knows how to live within a budget, and understands the pitfalls of using credit. Start giving weekly allowance and let your child draw up a budget that you will monitor/supervise. Budgeting skills help teenagers learn the value of money, conscious spending, as well as planning for the future. Financial discipline is an important skill to learn.

8.   Interpersonal skills

These help us to relate in positive ways with the people we interact with. This may mean being able to make and keep friendly relationships, which can be of great importance to our mental and social wellbeing. It may mean keeping good relations with family members, which are an important source of social support. It may also mean being able to end relationships constructively.

9.   Social Etiquette

Teaching your child skills and manners that they should display in social settings is essential for them to have a smooth social life. Start by teaching them the basic magic words: thank you, please, excuse me, sorry and pardon me. Having social skills opens great doors.

10.   Time management

Start by modelling good time management habits. If you are always wishing for more time and doing things in a hurry, chances are your children will learn to do that too.

Teach them to organise their time using a simple timetable or a planner. Let them create a schedule and stick to it. Even the slightest deviation from the plan can leave them crunched for time. Teach your children to prioritise their tasks, to use their time responsibly. Help them identify important tasks, and differentiate between what is important and what is urgent. Developing a routine makes it easier to manage time.

11.   Navigational skills

Basic navigational skills are important so that even if they do not have a car, they can travel from one place to another without being stranded. Some things they could learn include: being able to travel on bus, train or flight, being able to read their schedule and timetables, knowing traffic and road terms like curves, exits, freeways, highways, etc. and being aware of information about the different transport options to reach different places.

When my husband suggested that our sons learn how to navigate/move around in Nigeria, I almost panicked. But it was a great move because it made life easier for me and for them -- they can go anywhere using any means of transportation. What I tell the parents I coach is that these children will be leaving home soon, and they need to prepare them for the unknown and the known.

12.   Employability

Most vacations, my adolescents work in my store and they man different desks. This is to expose them to work and to help them learn some skills on the job. Another thing we did for my children is to let them go for internships at offices related to their career paths. This was to let them have a feel of their career choice before going to the university.

13.   Decision making

This skill is aided by critical thinking. It is a skill that can help an adolescent deal constructively with decisions about their life. Young adults can learn to assess the different options available to them, and consider what effects these different decisions are likely to have. If you have a child who is always indecisive, help him/her to start making small decisions like what food he/she would like to eat, what he/she wants to do, etc. For some children, it is fear that causes this indecision.

14.   Goal Setting

Teach your children to identify their skills and set goals that can give them personal gratification as well as professional success. In my home, we encourage our children to have a vision board where they set goals in different areas of their lives. This gives them a sense of purpose. You could teach yours to figure out what they want to do and where they want to be in a few years' time. Help them gain clarity. Set realistic goals using the SMART parameters.

15.   Personal and home maintenance

Grooming is a skill that your adolescent should learn early. Personal grooming is important to stay healthy. Teach them healthy habits like brushing and bathing daily. Explain the importance of keeping their body clean. They must know how to care for their skin and hair. (Most adolescents get into a hygiene routine during their identity formation stage.)

Teach your child how to manage utilities, pay bills, etc. Basic maintenance of the house: Teach them to vacuum, dust and clean the house. Simple things like fixing a broken circuit, locating a water valve and turning it off or on, and addressing the basic plumbing issues might help them to manage their house better. Teach them the simple rule of Kaizen – a place for everything and everything in its place. Teach them to change a car tyre, maintain a car, etc

Value development

Values are what we believe is right or wrong, these beliefs are important because they guide our decisions and actions. Your values will shape what you consider to be acceptable public conduct, work ethics and social views.Its very important you start your value clarification process earlier, by the time they are in their late adolescents they would have internalized them.

It's very important that your children are well equipped and grounded before they leave home for independent living.

CHAPTER 10

CONCLUSION

Wow! What a journey getting to know how to understand and connect with your adolescent. If your relationship with your teenager has been broken, I know with the help of God and with the steps I have shared in this book, it will be restored.

Raising children is a great responsibility that you have to be deliberate about. There is no quick fix to raising children into well-balanced adults; it is a journey and a process. This process starts from when your child is an infant, to adulthood. You have 18 years to teach, guide, lead and prepare them for adulthood and independent living. At the end of these 18 years, would you feel comfortable to release your child, knowing you have instilled all the right values, skills, knowledge and training?

Let your parenting journey start with the end in mind. What type of adult do you see? What type of future do you see for your child? Do you currently have all it takes to raise that adult you see? Start this process by working on areas you need to improve on. Is there any skill you need in becoming the best?

Well, you have lots of resources you can use; you can enlist the services of a coach for areas you need to develop in. You can also get a teen mentor for your adolescent -- someone whom you can trust, who also shares the same values with you.

Having a growth mindset is very important on this parenting journey. It helps you to keep improving and keep developing yourself; it also helps you to keep developing your children.

Thank you for buying and reading this book.

Oluwatoyin Ogunkanmi

Reference

1. Oluwatoyin Ogunkanmi - Smart Parenting, raising your child without losing your cool.

2. Oluwatoyin Ogunkanmi- No Yelling Guide

3. Oluwatoyin Ogunkanmi- Talk about Sex

4. Eril Erikson Psychosocial stages of development

5. Daniel J. Siegel- Brainstorm

6. Gary Chapman and Ross Campbell- The 5 Love Languages Of Children

7. Positive Paychology.com

8. Louise Clarke- Parenting the modern teen

9. Rhonda Stoppe- moms raising sons to men

10. Gottman- Raising emotionally intelligent child

11. Launching your kids for life - Bob &Cheryl Reccord

To get any accurate assessment done, please use the address on the last page of this book for a one-on-one coaching session with me.

To contact the author

For PUBLIC SPEAKING ENGAGEMENT,

COACHING AND TRAINING

Email address:
oluwatoyin@oluwatoyinogunkanmi.com

Instagram :oluwatoyinogunkanmi

Facebook:oluwatoyin ogunkanmi

Twitter : ttogunkanmi